Getting Ready for Winter

by Jeffery L. Williams

HAMERAY
PUBLISHING GROUP

Published in the United States of America
by the Hameray Publishing Group, Inc.

Copyright © 2016 Hameray Publishing Group, Inc.

Publisher: Raymond Yuen
Editor: Tara Rodriquez
Cover Designer: Anita Adams
Book Designer: Stephani Rosenstein

Photo Credits: Page i – Samuel Borges Photography;
Page 2 – Raymond Kasprzak; Page 3 – Heiko Kiera; Page 4 – Bruce
MacQueen; Page 5 – Tao Wang; Page 6 – Anne Kitzman; Page 7 – Neil
Burton; Page 8 – Tom Middleton; Page 9 – Steve Oehlenschlager;
Page 10 – Konrad Mostert; Page 11 – Leonardo Gonzalez;
Page 12 – Foto Ivan Kebe; Page 13 – Tyler Olson; Page 14 – Margaret
M. Stewart, Legna69 (inset); Page 15 – Monkey Business Images;
Page 16 – XiXinXing

ISBN 978-1-62817-581-3

Printed in China

1 2 3 4 5 6 7 IPS 22 21 20 19 18 17 16

Table of Contents

Animals have different ways to get ready for winter. They do this to **survive**.

Gathering Food

Some animals look for food to keep or store for winter.
Squirrels look for nuts and seeds.

Chipmunks also look for nuts and seeds.

Beavers look for branches
with leaves.

Building a Home

Some animals build a home for winter. Squirrels build a nest of leaves in a tree.

Mice dig a **burrow** in the ground.

Beavers build a **lodge** in a pond.

Going Away

Some animals go away for the winter. Geese fly far away to be where it is warm.

Whales swim far away to be
where it is warm.

Fish go deeper into the ocean, where it is warmer.

Going to Sleep

Some animals go to sleep for the winter. This is called **hibernating**. Snakes sleep under rocks or logs.

Bears sleep in caves.

Chipmunks sleep in burrows.

People

People get ready for winter too. We put on boots to go in the snow.

We put on coats to keep warm.
We put on gloves to keep our
hands warm. We stay in our
houses when it is too cold.

Glossary

burrow: a hole in the ground that an animal lives in

hibernating: going to sleep for the winter

lodge: a type of home that beavers build that is made of branches

survive: to stay alive

Index